Stable Stories

Stable Stories

the Sequel to TALES FROM THE SADDLE

Howard Green

Writers Club Press
New York Lincoln Shanghai

Stable Stories
the Sequel to TALES FROM THE SADDLE

Writers Club Press
an imprint of iUniverse, Inc.

For information address:
iUniverse
2021 Pine Lake Road, Suite 100
Lincoln, NE 68512
www.iuniverse.com

ISBN: 0-595-26521-9

Printed in the United States of America

Dedicated to my wife, Margery; and my children, Randell, Sharnell, Ron, Sharon & Shirley.

Contents

Forword

I remember when I was just a young child. I was out in the yard with two of my brothers, and we were playing "Cowboy and Indian," and the conversation came up—what were we going to grow up to be.... And I remember this like it was yesterday...and it was probably a hundred years ago, that I said I was going to grow up to be a cowboy and a church member. I achieved the first part. The latter part maybe will come in future years.

Yesterday I received copies of my first book, "Tales from the Saddle." It's kind of exciting. Today I've autographed a few of them and carried them around to some of my special friends—and you know me, I'm going to be gloating about it.

When I first kind of decided that I wanted to write a book, my first book, friends and acquaintances kind of said, "Yeah, right, go ahead, but don't give up your day job."

A copy of "Tales from the Saddle" got to a gentleman in England who was a graduate from Oxford University. And he read this book, and he critiqued it to my wife, and he thought the book was great and just elaborated on a lot of things, and I was so impressed with this. Me, just a little old cowboy, spent my life mainly with horses...to be, I guess I would say "honored," a lot of real nice comments made by this gentleman who was a graduate of Oxford and then a teacher...er, it just crosses my mind a lot of times. I just keep talking about how impressed I was to get a critique like this from this gentleman, because he's well educated and plumb across the ocean from me. And for him to comment like he did has left a lasting memory with me. Again, I'm so impressed, will always be impressed, and I've never met the gentlemen...sure would like to...and all the time it took to write this book was real worthwhile to get a comment from a gentleman of his stature.

....

I'm in the process of writing 2 other books, and when these books are finished and published, I will make every effort to see that this gentleman in England gets copies. And I hope his critiques will be as pleasant as my first book.

Well, I did the first book, and now I'm on the second one; and sure, I'd like for the books to make money, I'd like that very much. However, if it does not, all is not lost because I feel that some of the knowledge I can pass on to the younger generation while I'm still here on earth…it might help them down the road somewhere.

There's too many people that, during their lifetime, build up a lot of knowledge…know about certain things…and when they're gone, all the knowledge is gone with them. I don't want to do this. I want to pass on any knowledge that might be beneficial to any of the people left on earth after I'm gone, and I feel that I do have a lot of good knowledge to pass on–and I'll keep all the bad knowledge to myself…!

Introduction

In my book, "Tales from the Saddle," at the end of it, I made a statement that you all come back and see us—that I should be around for a little while longer. Well, that's changed...I guess you'd call this an end of an era. I'm no longer associated with a riding stable or a dude ranch. I made that final not too long ago, and people ask me, "Do you miss the stable business?" And my remark is: "Gladly." It seems to me like I was in that business for a hundred years or more. Yes, I do miss some of it, and yes, I'm glad to miss some of it...but it's time for a new trail, and I'm looking forward to riding down that very shortly.

We all know that we're the last of the dying breed, and we know that our best days are gone. So, we'll just have to take one day at a time, go on down the trail, and take what life deals out to us.

I might not be associated with the riding stable business anymore, but Lord, there's a lot of memories that need to be told–some good, some bad, and some just in between. But as I go down the trail, I'm going to try to remember all this stuff that I missed in my first book, and I'm going to try to bring it all to you.

I've had a lot of offers from people from Arkansas, Canada, and various other places…asking me to move out where they were at and enjoy the rest of my time. My answer to them was I think I've waited too late and that I'm just going to have to stay here in Arizona…fight the desert heat, beat on the rock, and hope something good'll come out of it.

When I was running a riding stable or working in a riding the stable, my day was always planned for me. I knew where I had to be and what I had to do. Now that I am no longer operating the stable, I have to search for things to do and kind of plan my day to where I can be doing something constructive. People ask me, "Are you glad you're retired?" My response is, "I'm not retired."

Life goes on without running a stable. I still have my horses around me, and I think that if I woke up in the morning and didn't have a horse on the place, I wouldn't be comfortable at all. Rarely do I ride anymore; rarely do I do anything with the horses. But just seeing them out in the pasture, knowing I have to feed them a couple of times a day and look after them gives me a feeling of contentment.

If you ever find yourself really depressed, wound up real tight and don't know what to do about it, try unwinding on horseback. Go rent, borrow, beg, or steal (not really!) your(self) a horse, get on him, and ride across country. Just get out by yourself where you don't hear anything but nature. I guarantee that when you spend some time that way, you'll come back more relaxed than you would if you went to every doctor in the United States. Don't ask me how it works. I just know it's worked for me several times, and you just have to go and find out for yourself. And I know...I know the relaxed feeling is what a person needs, and I've found so much relaxation just doing things with a horse.

Now that I don't operate a stable anymore, when I leave my house in the mornings, I really don't know where I'm going. I have no place I really need to be, but I'm always looking and thinking that if I look the right way and turn my truck wheel the right way that I'll run into a new adventure or something that I've never done and something that I'd want to do. And good things will always turn out for you if you maintain this type of mind.

I (do) go by my old stable probably once a week or every 2 weeks or whatnot…a lot of good memories there (and) a lot of bad memories…. But I think the good outweighed the bad, and I guess, to tell anybody the truth, I wouldn't mind being associated with a stable again, because there's so much about it that I miss.

Observations on Life

As I ride along this morning (and) look out into the desert, you wonder how many recorded, how many unrecorded deaths it took to settle this territory. They had to fight all the elements, such as heat, the cold, Indian raids, robbers, about anything you can think of...they fought it, they coped with it, they did it. I just wonder today how many people could go through the same thing that these people went through to settle this territory and survive. We've got to remember that they didn't have any ice. They didn't have any electric. They didn't have heat...only what wood they would cut to build fires at night. They couldn't sleep well—thinking they might get killed during the night–so it took a really special type of people to conquer this desert and the Arizona territory. My hats are off to them.

The Arizona sunset
Is a lovely sight to see
When the sun sets in the evenings
It leaves lasting memories

You can hear the coyotes howling
As the sun sets in the west
Yes, the Arizona desert
Is the place that I love best

You can find beauty all around you
And you don't have far to go
You don't worry about it raining
And there is never fear of snow

The desert and its wonders
Will steal your heart away

So don't come to Arizona
Unless you are planning a long stay.

******

Today, people are running up and down the highways...in big fancy cars, drinking finest whisky...a lot of them never, never give one thought to how they were able to do this. If it hadn't been for the ancestors...our ancestors in the past and suffering they went through, and let's not forget the horse. The horse and the people made it possible for this fellow to run up and down the road in a big, fine car at a hundred miles an hour, but they never stop to think who and what made this possible. It all boils down to one thing, the horse.

There's thousands of people that built their empires...became millionaires...built a nice, comfortable life for them and their family...and how many of them do you think realize that the horse, well, in some way or another, it helped them gain this fame? I doubt if you'll find one in all the group who'll give any credit to the horse. I don't think you could find anybody that's wealthy, or famous, or whatever, that if you looked back in history far enough that a horse didn't help them gain this fame. But it will continue to happen, the horse will be forgotten. People will go on with their lifestyles...never realizing that the horse and the special breed of people that used this horse properly brought the West together and created all the nice things that people have today.

You know, I guess I'm kind of living in no man's land. I don't like the way things are going today, and I know I can't turn back the clock and make them they way I wanted them to go like it was years ago. I see these people, they just ride your bumper, you're driving the speed limit, and they're riding up on your back. They're always in a hurry to get somewhere, and once they get there, they don't have one idea how they got there and why they had to get there that fast.

I guess I'm luckier than most. I had my life with the horse, mostly all at a slow pace, and I was in no hurry to get anywhere. People nowadays in this rapid pace they're setting will never realize how much they missed by not slowing life down and just taking the pace that I did as the horse wanted to go. Again, I say that I'm very fortunate. I got to do things that the current generation will never do.

Airplanes fly across the sky
And cars speed down the street
People are so busy
They rarely stop to eat

They love their life in the fast lane
They never have time to wait

They are in a hurry to go nowhere
And don't want to be late

Oh, how wonderful it would be
If we all slow down our pace
And move along in the slow lane
Not trying to win a race.

******

Here's another little joke, a little poem I guess you would say, that fits most of the people out on these highways nowadays, and it goes something like this:

I don't know where I'm going
And I don't know where I've been
But if I get there
I'd want to go back again.

So, that's just about the way they handle them-selves on the road, don't know where they're going, want to hurry up and get there so they can go again.

Had a funny thing happen to me the other day when I went into town. On my way, I got to cramping, so I just kind of unbuckled my belt and the top of the zip of my pants to give my stomach some room and drove on into town. I stopped at a convenience store, and–not think-ing–I just stepped out of the car. And would you believe my pants fell all they way down to my ankles...?! I'd forgotten to buckle up before I got out. Well, anyway, I looked around, grabbed my pants, and pulled 'em up...and you know, there was a heck of a lot of people there, and no one even noticed me! They were in that big (of) a rush, so I got away with that one!

Arizona, Technology & Politics (& the horse)

Today was the first day of summer. A lot of people (were) complaining how hot it is. Well, heck, it's hot about every day in Arizona. If they can't get along with the heat, there is a way out–you move. The majority of Arizona is made up of people from out-of-state, and they will constantly complain about the heat. One day, I asked an individual, "Did you ever see me shovel sunshine away from my doorstep?" Meaning, they'd been shoveling snow, and you never have to shovel sunshine, so why complain about it?

Summer's here, and it's sure as hell hot
I'd take me a nap, but I don't have a cot
All I can do is sit here and think
Once in a while go get me a drink

Winter comes; it'll bring new days
Right now, it seems that's far, far away
I'm sitting here busted, don't have a buck
Hoping tomorrow will bring me better luck.

******

I rode down from Amarillo trying to escape the
things I'd done
Wound up in a place they call "Valley of the Sun"
I stayed there until the summer, and boy, it got
really hot

I looked all over the Valley trying to find a
shady spot
I made myself a promise, if I get through all
this sweat
I won't be here next year, that you sure can bet!

******

We had a power outage the night before last–out for about 8 hours. I didn't think I was going to get through it. The heat was bothering me so bad—it was 116 degrees Fahrenheit–and here, no power for 8 hours. I like to went nuts, but then I thought back to the people who came out and settled this place here...how in the world did they do it? How in the world did they survive all the heat (with) no ice, no cold water, no air conditioning? But they survived, they settled, they stayed; and as I've said many times, this had to be one special breed of tough people. Anybody who could handle a situation like that...survive, build, and make the land around them grow...they're just to be admired. There's no other way of saying it, they were just special, special people.

******

We have several thousand people a day moving into the state of Arizona. It seems like every one of them who gets a house...they've got to have a real green lawn, water it daily, and keep it all correct. I've often, well, I've always thought that the Arizona landscaping with all the new houses, old houses, or whatever, should be desert landscaping–due to the fact we don't have a lot of water. But I'm sure that people a hell of a lot smarter than I am have figured out why they should have green lawns instead of desert landscaping. The golf courses and all should be desert landscaping to preserve water for the future because we don't have a lot to spare....

******

It's 6 a.m., a beautiful morning...it's quiet, peaceful, the birds are singing. Just sitting out here and enjoying the day before all the hustle and bustle begins. Went out to feed my horses—they were back in the pasture–put the feed out, they didn't even want to come in, because the trees have so many mesquite beans on them. They're enjoying the mesquite beans and don't really care about regular feed when the beans are in season. However, the horses, they've started, now, to come in. I have one horse here that will eat 26 hours a day if you let her. This is her main hobby–eating–and she will let you know if there's no food around.

I moved out to this place where I'm living about 16 years ago. There was hardly anyone around, except me and my family, and now I look out across the fields and across the desert from my house…and there's nothing but houses, trailers, a tremendous amount of building going on. And I know you can't stand in the way of progress, but it kind of gives you a sad feeling to see all the beautiful land and desert vegetation go into housing. Plants have such a struggle to survive in the desert, and if they've succeeded in keeping a tenuous hold on life, it seems a shame to make their struggle worthless. Newcomers will often remove all the vegetation from their plot of land and then either leave it barren or plant non-desert trees, etc. and grass. I'm all in favor of grass, but as it takes more water per week to keep it green than this area's rainfall for an entire year, it's hard to justify planting grass. If there's enough rain at one time, grass appears by itself (ask rainy place gardeners who are always having to pull it up out of their flower gardens!), even in the desert. And if there isn't enough rain, it stays dormant. Of course, part of the argument for clearing land around new houses is because of the always-present likelihood of fire. But even firefighters differentiate between clearing out dead, dry brush–the fire hazard–and leaving living trees and bushes, which provide shade. Unfortunately, all too many people remove everything. And although there are now unused-for-crops fields out here (which no doubt originally were desert and in their time were cleared) as well as desert, it seems that it is the desert rather than the fields that are more attractive for building, so more desert is being destroyed. I'm not guilty of hypocrisy. I moved into a house that was already here, and I planted eucalyptus trees–that don't need much water–for shade, and (I) let the desert bushes grow back.

You drive down the highway; you look out across the desert, and everybody's saying, "Oh, how beautiful the desert is," and "how beautiful" this and "how beautiful" that. They'll stop and take pictures of all the beauty and everything. True, the desert is very beautiful, but desert is ever changing, and if you ride out into the desert today and ride out again tomorrow, it'll never be the same. The desert changes overnight...the flowers, the shrubbery, everything. But the desert is (also) very deceiving, it can be very cruel. You can freeze at night, and you can burn during the day. You can have nothing but dust, or torrential rain. So, again, my hat's off to the very special people who conquered, stayed, survived and made it grow.

******

In Arizona, you don't have a lot of pasture, other than certain times of the season, like it is back east where you've got green fields you can turn your animals out on and the cost of feed is very little. But here in Arizona, you've got to buy everything that your animals get; and with the way prices are going on up now, in some cases the horses will get less to eat, because the people that own horses can't afford to buy the feed. I often tell people when they're buying horses (that) the initial cost of one is not as great as the upkeep. There's the feed, the worming, the shoe-ing, the general health and condition that you've got to watch over...and people will run out and buy a horse, thinking that they can feed him like you would a dog. And that's where a lot of these horses get down on their weight, and it's very hard with an older horse (particularly) to bring him back. A lot of people will come and want to buy a horse on installment plans. This is no good. If a person can't afford the price of a horse, you know darn well that they can't afford to feed him and take care of him properly.

Along the same subject, riding through the Indian reservation, occasionally you will see a band of horses running free. They are enjoying themselves with nobody to abuse them...they're fat, pretty, just putting on a good show for the people when they go by...running out into the wild, the way they're supposed to be, not to be mishandled or abused. And if you do take a horse, you doggone sure should take good care of him and not let anyone abuse this animal, because he wasn't put on this earth to be abused. He was put on this earth to help us get where we are today.

After seeing these Indian horses running wild and free, then you wonder why our government spends millions to gather these horses up and then let someone adopt them who doesn't have a clue about what they're getting (themselves) into. And who ends up doing all the suffering? It's the horse, and our government does this every year–rounds up a big herd and puts them up for adoption all over the United States. And 90% of the people wind up letting the horses feet go and everything, and nothing is done with them...eventually, they're going to wind up in slaughter, because they can't train this horse the way they should be trained for domestic use. Our government is doing great things, and I hope they pat themselves on the back and are real proud of what they're doing, because it ain't working (the way) they think it's working, and all it does is create a bunch of unnecessary jobs. They pay big money out, and who winds up paying the bills? The taxpayer, and is that fair? No.

The government is forgetting one important thing about the horse. In the past, the horse was the only means for the army…(even) transportation for the army. They carried food, they carried the soldiers, they took them into war, and they even took care of them during peace. But now that they're no longer needed, they're throwing them out to the mercy of these people that don't need these horses and wouldn't take these horses unless the government were advertising and want them to be wherever they're having their adoption deal. And all they guarantee you is when you get this horse, they'll put a halter on it, (they'll) run it in a chute and put a halter on it, and (they'll) load him in a trailer for you. Then you're on your own. It ain't right, and I'll continue to holler–probably never do any good–but I don't like what our government is doing to the horse when the horse took care of them in the past...several thousand years, we could say. But I know the horse was still used as of up till...the horse and the mule were used up until World War II. It ain't right, folks.

Let me go back to this Bureau of Land Management thing. They take, I don't know, hundreds of people, probably, to do all of this gathering and corralling and tagging and everything, getting these horses ready for adoption. My theory would be if they're going to put these horses up for adoption, like I've said before, qualify people. But you know they're not going to do that. And I'll venture to say that out of every 20 horses that they put up for adoption, they don't have one qualified person that knows how to deal with this horse. But yet, if they've got property, they're going to do it. What I'm saying is these horses would be better off if they just went up on the range where they gather 'em...and just shoot 'em instead of putting them into the slow abuse that they're doing with it when they put them up for adoption. To me, I'm not in favor of either. I'm not in favor of shooting a horse, but I'm (also) not in favor of adopting to people who have no knowledge, because they've got to keep this horse for a year before they can get rid of it. And from the unqualified person, that horse is not going to get the proper care. He will be totally abused for a year or more if they keep him longer than that.

You know, the Bureau of Land Management, they'll come and they'll announce the day they're going to have these adoptions and so forth...and after the adoption, maybe they adopted out 20, 30, maybe a hundred. And they'll pat each other on the back and say what a great job they did.

You know, it cost millions to gather these horses and get them ready for adoption. They probably brought in $5,000 for the state. Don't add up, does it? If nothing else, at least one of our many, many politicians should be smart enough to see the money difference...and that this thing is just not working. Why aren't they smart enough to see it?

The wild horse. They claim that the reason, one of the reasons, that they are out gathering them up for adoption and spending all these millions to do it is that sometimes the horses wander off onto the farmlands and do damage...or onto ranchland, doing damage to the grazing area. But if you get your pencil out and figure it up, it would be a hell of a lot cheaper to go and pay for these damages, leave the horse alone...rather than to do the things they're doing now—putting him in the hands of people who can't care for him.

******

It's a funny thing. I'm supposed to be talking about horses and horse-related subjects in this book, but I broke down at a red-light this morning...called, had to wait for help pushing the vehicle and do all that good stuff. You wouldn't believe how many government vehicles went by...with women driving and 2 or 3 people in the vehicle and all of this stuff. Why in the heck do they, somebody who works for the government, get furnished a vehicle to get back and forth to work? These politicians are always looking for ways to spend money and not save money. If they want to save money, take these vehicles away from these people...they're misusing them out there anyhow.

You look out in the fields, and there are people working for $5 an hour. They don't have a vehicle to get to work in, and if you don't get to work, you'll get fired. Why is it that we're protecting these people working for the government, furnishing them everything and mileage and everything to go with it...and the rest of us have to struggle to get to our jobs, or we know very well that we won't have a job. Save money? If you'd go out and pull in all of these vehicles and get rid of the ones that shouldn't be used, and if the person can't get to work when working for the government, by golly, fire him. Get somebody who can get there. What I'll say is, it all winds up. When it winds up, that's why taxes get raised...because we're supporting a bunch of people with vehicles that we shouldn't be supporting. That's just one of the many things.

******

You know, since September 11th, there's been a lot of flag wavers, and they say the people have all come together and all of this. Maybe so. I don't know, but I do know this much: that 50% of the people who are waving these flags have no idea why they're waving a flag. They should go back and read their history books and see just how important it is to wave this flag...and what it (the flag) means. You've got to earn the right to wave this flag freely. I know, I've fought for this flag, and I respect the flag. And I just hope that one day, these people who're waving Old Glory will go back into the books and read, and find out what it really means. And then they can wave the flag and really believe what they're doing. But until then, I think a lot of people are just waving flags and tying them on the car just to attract attention.

******

We have livestock all over the place—several of the people around us do—and Arizona just passed a law that it's illegal to shoot weapons in the air. But (there are holidays–namely New Year's Eve–where) everyone out here was shooting their weapons up in the air with no regard as to where the bullet might land. How in the world can you teach these ignorant people that it's illegal...it's dangerous...and it could kill somebody by shooting these guns into the air. Why pass a law if we don't enforce it? There was no enforcement in the area.

To elaborate further on this so-called new law that they passed about shooting guns off near houses or within the city limits, this law was already on the books, and it's not enforced. But the politicians are (once again) patting themselves on the back and saying what a good job they did to pass this law about shooting your guns in the air. No law is any good unless it's enforced, and all the politicians do is go out and make some new laws and then just file it away, and they feel that they've done a great job. To me, they've done nothing…nothing but keep smothering America with paperwork. It's time that people stood up and made these politicians do what they say they're going to do. This is not happening. One day, we're going to regret all this, and we're stupid enough to go and elect these same politicians that did nothing and elect them to another term. What's going on here? What are we doing? It's time to stand up and make these people do what they say they're going to do, or don't put them in office.

I'm getting way off track from the book, getting way off track from what the book is supposed to be about, so I'd better get off this politician kick. It irritates me just to talk about it…you see what's going on, but you can't do anything about it…so, I'll go back to talking about something that I really love and enjoy, the ol' horse.

******

Yesterday, whilst loading some horses, I had my mind on other things...not paying attention, I hit my head on the trailer door...knocked myself about half-silly–or should I say, a bit sillier than I am. Almost got trampled, but my point is this: when you're handling horses, your mind's got to be on that horse. Your mind can't be off in some other area or the same thing will happen to you that it did me, and it's not fun.

Horses have an uncanny ability to know the instant a person's mind wanders, and some of them are quick to take advantage. Most people who ride have stories to tell of the times they let their minds wander and ended up hanging from the branches of a tree, or in some other predicament. Horses know just how much space they take up, and they know that the rider takes more...and they can be quick to remind a non-attentive rider that it's a good idea to pay attention. (It's) Safer, too, because sometimes the horses needs instant help.

******

The other day, I saw a girl riding a horse out at one of the arenas. The horse was gimping in his right front—you could see he was hurting—you could tell. I told her, I said, "You ought to do something about that, you know. Get a vet to check him or something, because the horse ain't right, he's gimping." She said, "Oh, my horse doesn't gimp, he's gaited." Well, if that's the case, I see a lot of people riding gaited horses nowadays.

******

You know, if the doggone old horse didn't have enough to worry about with all the things I've talked about earlier (and will talk about in the future, I'm sure), now they've got a new deal going, and it consists of women...they'll come around to your place, you've got a horse for sale or whatever the case may be....and they'll try to talk you into donating it to the animal rescue and that they will find a good home for it and it'll be cared for real good. You won't want to believe this, but after you make this donation, you will find (that) in a week or 2, this horse will be (at) a livestock sale...that everything goes into this woman's pocket, all profit. When they tell you they're from animal rescue, you'd better do a lot of checking, because there's 3 or 4 women out there now who're pulling this soft soap act on people and getting them to donate their horse–thinking they're doing the right thing. However, I know better, and so do several other people. These horses wind up on the sale block, and they could go anywhere from slaughter to a good home to a bad home...but my point is, these people are conning others out of their horses and then making a sizeable profit. It should not be tolerated, and it will go on, because nobody cares enough to go and look into it. But what I was saying earlier, (if) the horse didn't have enough to worry about–by golly, here's more.

******

Unexpectedly, I had a phone call from one of my old roping buddies down in Sierra Vista, and we reminisced for a long time. He and I had the fastest time at the rodeo, roping, and got a standing ovation–which I'll never forget. And he brought me up to date on all the old boys I used to rope with and was in the Sheriff's Posse together with...and how many of them had died and passed on. It kind of makes you realize how old you're getting...how much time you've got left.

(I also realize) It's sure hard for me to get used to this high-tech life. I remember back when I was growing up that when you had a problem—like if you had hay in the field that needed to be gathered...or if you had corn that needed to be gathered, or anything–the neighbors would come from miles away to help you do this. They didn't expect to be paid for it. They would spend hours, they would drive with a team and wagon, or ride a horse to get to where you lived–probably took 3 or 4 hours to get there, but they didn't mind a bit. They would come and help you with any problems you had; and of course you would do that for them, too, if they ever let you know (that) they needed help. Nowadays, when people come to your house, you know they're not coming to help you–I'm speaking of the majority, there are some exceptions. But nowadays, you worry about if they're going to rip you off or possibly kill you. So I prefer the olden days to the present, being an old-timer myself.

I know that people will be people, and they're going to act the way most everybody does in this day and time. But I do have a feeling that one day the big man up in the sky, the big man upstairs is going to stand up and say, "I've had my fill of the way you people are acting and ignoring and defying and I think I'm just going to put a stop to it." And I think that's when we're going to see a whole new change...maybe a whole new world...and I will probably never see (it). But I'm thinking that not in the too distant future the man upstairs is going to stand up and be accounted (for)...and let everybody know what his feelings are, having every rule that he put on this earth defied and abused.

I heard a news commentator just the other night on TV raising all kinds of cain about how we've destroyed the ozone and how everything is going to come to an end within a few years due to all the vehicles and pollution/(pollutants). You know, if I can recall correctly, when our 4-legged friend was a major part of our transportation, I don't believe I ever heard any-body comment about pollution.

A lot of old cowboys and ranchers, including myself, look around every day and wonder what happened to their main mode of transporta-tion...and I can also say, their lifeline. This has been destroyed right in front of our eyes, and there's nothing we can do about it. It's really a sad situation–to depend on something as all the old cowboys did, and then have to sit by when you're old, feeble and disabled to watch this beautiful animal being either misused, abused, or destroyed. God help us all.

Do we applaud the high-tech world that we're in today, or do we curse it?

Memories

I remember when I was down in the Sierra Vista area, you know, just being a plain old country boy and not expecting much out of life...to get involved in the stable business and ranch business, to make contact, rub shoulders, communicate with so many celebrities.... It's kind of an unbelievable story, but this happened to me. I didn't go out looking for it. It just came to me in the type of work I was doing. So, it goes to show you, if you're working at the right place, at the right stable, good things will come your way. And so will memories that will last forever.

******

I stopped one day to help a friend of mine deliver a calf. The cow was having problems, and we had to pull the calf to get it out…get the cow up and take care of the calf…and in a few minutes, everything was pretty normal. The calf was nursing, and everything appeared to be just fine.

Then, I guess you'd call it–I had a flashback, or a delayed remembrance, or whatever you want to call it. But I thought about the time, years ago, back in Germany, when I was a member of the military police. My partner and I were out patrolling in a little town outside of Frankfurt, and we came up on this woman who appeared to be drunk or having some kind of difficulties. We got her into the jeep and took her over to our police station. (We) came to find out she was in labor and fixing to have a baby, so we put her on a bench–where we usually made the prisoners sit when we brought them in–and we gave her a rolled up comic book for her to bite on, and (we) went ahead and delivered her baby. And then we called the German hospital, and they came over and picked up her and the baby, and they were doing real good. I guess we did all the right things, but anyhow, this story goes further. The lady wound up naming the baby after my partner and I (good thing it was a boy!), and later, we made the local newspapers there. And then, shortly after that, we had an interview with a prestigious publication who did print the article about us delivering a baby. And that kind of made my head get big at that time. It's a real fond memory about the whole thing.

******

I was a member of a Sheriff's Posse group (as I mentioned earlier), and we rode in quite a few parades. And I recall one that I rode in...it was Rex Allen Days, and the star himself had come over to ride in the parade and promote the rodeo, which is an annual event in Wilcox,

Arizona. At that time, there was a serious type of horse disease going on, and I believe it was called V double E, and they wouldn't let the star bring his horse across the border. So, he came on over with another famous movie star, and when the parade got ready to go, the 2 of them walked right in front of our group...all the whole parade route, shaking hands with people and greeting people all the way to the rodeo grounds. It was quite a deal to be up close with famous people like that and see how down to earth they were when it came to meeting the ordinary person. And I'll never forget that, because we offered them horses to ride, and they said, "no," and went ahead and just walked the entire parade. Everybody sure enjoyed it.

******

They have this parade in Tombstone called Helldorado Days. I had a good friend down in Sierra Vista who was the DJ for the country and western shows that they did at that station. Then there were 2 young ladies, neither of them had ever ridden in a parade of any type, and they kept bugging me to get Dick and everybody and we'd go ride in the parade. And finally I agreed to it, and the 2 girls carried a banner advertising this country and western DJ and that station that he worked for. I rode in front of the banner on a stallion I had by the name of Little Comanche B, who was totally nervous...couldn't keep him stopped or sitting still at any time...you'd have to circle him when they wanted to stop. I'd have to go in circles 'till we were ready to go again in order to keep him from throwing a fit. But anyway, we completed the ride, and everybody was excited and happy, and this DJ enjoyed it so much, because he'd never been able to participate in any type of parade with horses. And he couldn't thank me enough. Well, later on, he got transferred to Phoenix to one of those main country and western stations. And one day, I had my radio tuned to that station. I was driving down the road, and this gentleman came on the air and said that he wanted to play a special song for Howard Green for allowing him to ride in this parade...for furnishing the horses. And he said that it was the greatest time he'd ever had and that he'd never forget it. And he played a song for me, and that really, really meant a lot to me.

******

I knew this girl down in Tucson, a blonde-headed girl about 20 years old, and pretty as a picture. She had leukemia, and she had a very short time to live; and she had kind of fell in love with an appaloosa stud that I had by the name of Little Comanche B, kind of a sharp-looking horse. And her desire was that she got to ride this stud horse in the Tucson Parade. I was kind of reluctant at first, although she was a pretty good hand with a horse. I didn't think she'd be stout enough to keep this horse in tow whilst all the activity was going on around him, but finally, I agreed. I hauled the horse up to Tucson and met this young lady and took her with me over to the starting place of the parade. Got her all mounted up and everything, got her number spot, and the parade took off. I drove around to meet her at the other end of the parade route with the horse-trailer. She came through with flying colors and handled the horse perfectly, and she was so excited (that) she could hardly talk. But I was glad I did it, because a very short time after that, she passed away. I really felt good about being part of this young lady's–you might say, last wish....that I was instrumental in helping her have a good time and enjoy herself and get to do one of the goals that she wanted to do before she died. So, all in all, I feel that I did do a little bit of good.

******

I recall a western movie that was filmed down in Old Tucson. It was a series, and in fact, the house and everything that was used for the ranch headquarters, to the best of my knowledge, is still standing at Old Tucson. This was a great group of people…got to know most of the cast pretty well and even rode in the Tucson rodeo parade with them. And, boy, did the jokes fly. I mean, they were all a fun-loving bunch, and we had fun all through the parade and after. I used to go out to the set and hang out, sometimes take horses; and most of the time, I was seeing if I could get on as an extra and then seeing if I could lease out some of my horses to them. This went on for quite a spell, and finally the series came to an end. I lost track of everybody, but this was a great time in my life, and I really enjoyed it.

There was another western filmed down in Tucson, and the main character had a series of his own, prior to filming this film, that lasted approximately 20 years. A real fine gentleman, easy to talk to and wasn't stuck up. It was a pleasure to go out on the set and just hang out.

******

You know, looking back to my days down in Tucson, I now see it as a time when my life was filled with a lot of great adventures, and I just probably didn't take the time to realize this and enjoy it as I should. But as I look back, I'm glad I got to do these things, and hopefully in the future, there'll be time for more.

******

Some years ago, me and a roping friend of mine was out tipping a few and having a good time one night. We were going from bar to bar, and we wound up in this one little old place— there was just him and I and a couple of other people—and then one old hippy boy was sitting at his bar, drinking beer, and his old hair down to his ankles.... And we (had) had a couple of drinks, and my friend said, "Why don't we give him a cowboy haircut?" And of course, I was feeling pretty good, and I said, "By golly, that sounds all right. (If) we had some clippers, we'd durn sure do it." And he said, "I just happen to have some out in my truck." He walked out the door and got them, and we called old hippy boy outside and kind of roached him. The police were called, and we left. But later on, about 2 days after that, we got stopped by the police and taken in and got a pretty good lecture over it, but that was all that happened.

Lost Night–Lost Job

Worked hard all day, the sun was still setting,
I was tired as hell, and I was still sweating,
Went into town to have me a beer,
The next thing I knew, I was flat on my ear,
Woke up next morning, I was feeling real bad,

And you know, I can't remember all the fun that
I had.
Drove back to the ranch and started loading hay,
The foreman came up, said, "Here is your pay,"
He said, "People here show up for work,
And we have no room for a big drunken jerk."

*****

Another friend of mine was roping one day, and when he got down just about the time to throw his row, his horse bobbed his head and started bucking...bucked him off and threw him right into the fence. This woman was sittin' on the front of her truck there, right where he was thrown off; and needless to say, the woman was no raving beauty in any respect. She ran over and picked this guys head up, trying to find out if he was all right. And he told me later that when he opened his eyes and looked up at that woman's face that he thought he'd died and gone to hell, 'cause he'd never seen anyone that ugly in his whole life.

******

I remember one time down in Sierra Vista, had a gymkhana going. (One of) My daughter(s) had a paint horse called Wendy (that) she thought the world of and did real good with. And I was one of the judges that day, and the old horse started giving her a little hard time, like he was bucking a little bit and not getting out there and doing the job he was supposed to. (So) I told her, "Bring that horse over to me, and let me straighten him out for you, and we'll get on with business."

She did, reluctantly—she didn't like for me to get on her horse–but anyway, I took the horse and took him out in the arena, put my spurs on and a riding crop, and I bathed him real good and took him around the arena a few times. (I) thought I had him straightened out, and there was a side gate right by the snack bar, and this gate had a crosstie on each side of it. This horse, I guess he'd had enough of me, and I'm loping him around the arena. And we got right about to that gate, he ducked a sharp left, and out the gate he went, catching my knee on one of the crossties. Then he lit into bucking again, and he bucked right up to my daughter and stopped and dropped his head right where she was...so, I never attempted to straighten her horse out for her again, and she got a big kick out of it.

Wreck on the River

Riding an old horse down by the river,
He spooked real bad and started to quiver.
I knew right then I was in for a wreck,
I will ride him out–what to heck.
He went straight up, then turned around,
All four feet hit hard on the ground.
I looked for a place where I could bail out,
But this horse had me figured out.

He went to the left and sharp to the right,
Me and this horse had a hell of a fight.
I guess he won, 'cause I'm here on the ground
Not looking forward to another round.

******

I was at a father/son, father/daughter roping in Sonora. Got through roping, went over to my truck, was going to sit down and just relax for a while until they called us again. And all of a sudden, I got terribly, terribly sick at the stomach, and I hollered for my daughter to help me go to the bathroom. Whilst I was in the bathroom, I passed out...and when I came to, someone had rolled me and taken my wallet and a lot of other personal stuff. Finally, when someone found me and helped me get up out of the bathroom and to their truck, the doctor was called. They put needles in my veins and started pumping stuff into me, and I was conscious, but sick. And after the doctor was through with me–we lived about 40 miles from where we were at–I laid down in the back of my truck, and some friends drove me home. There were some kids who rode in the back of my truck with me to make sure I'd be all right, and I do remember where you turn to go to my house. Er, well, anyway, when we got there, I was sleeping all this time in the back of the truck. And when we got to where we were supposed to turn to get to my house, well, there was this kid who rode with me in the truck...he shook me real hard, and I raised up real quick, and he said, "Howard, we're home." And when I woke up and looked out, all I could see was Hatfield's Funeral Home, and it scared me half to death! I told him the next day, "Don't you ever do something like that to me again." But after a few days recuperation, I was all right again, and I was informed by the doctors that I'd had a heat stroke; and you know, to this day, I get hot real quick. I've got to get into the shade, because once you've had a heat stroke, the heat affects you more severely than it would someone else. Oh, yes, if I remember correctly, I missed both steers–the one for my son, and the one for my daughter–and that didn't make me too popular either!

******

I remember one time my daughter, she was about 11 years old at the time, and she entered the Rodeo Queen's contest. Her horse was lame, and she had to use my big stud horse that we called Lucky Warrior to do her horsemanship part in this Queen's contest. The Queen contest consisted of 3 categories–poise, personality, and horsemanship. So, come time, she would have had to sit on the other side of the arena, away from the other contestants, because the ol' horse, the ol' stud horse that she was riding was kind of unruly at times. And I was keeping my fingers crossed that she could handle him. I used to rope on this horse and do various other things with him...and I could handle him, but sometimes he'd get out of line, and it took a pretty stout hand to straighten him up. So, she was sitting over by herself and waiting 'till her turn came. And when the announcer called for her to do her horsemanship part, she tore into that arena—running the barrels, did the starts, stops, spins, slide, everything that was on the program for her to do. And she came out of there (with) a big smile on her face, 'cause she new she'd done well. And I was totally relaxed, because I knew that she'd done well. And everybody, all of the contestants, after they'd done their part that they had to do, they lined up and waited to see what the results were. And whenever the announcer came up and said, "The winner is..." and gave my daughter's name, she rode into that arena so proud that she had done it on a big stud horse that nobody expected she could handle.

******

When we were attending all the gymkhana and rodeo events, my son and daughter used to be with me almost every event I went to. And I recall a lot of times when we'd go to some of the events and people would see our trailer pull in, I heard the remarks made, "Those Green kids are back here again." And I knew that by the time all the events were over that we would probably come out with most of the trophies, and I guess that's why all the other kids and adults kind of resented our presence.

******

I had a great big read roan horse that I used to rope on, and we called him Red Man. My (oldest) son at that time was very young, small, and this old horse was probably 16 hands high. And my son used to climb up on the fence and holler, "Red Man, come here," and the old horse would come over. And my son would get on him bareback and ride him around. We kept the old horse quite awhile, and then he got old...and there was this lady, an elderly lady, who wanted to get a horse. And I gave this horse to her, and she kept him right down the road from where we were. She had this old horse for quite a while, rode him on the trail rides and enjoyed him...and then, one morning, I went out to feed my horses. And this horse had got out and came to my place, right in front of my tack room, and lay down and died. I guess he knew where he wanted to die. My wife (at the time) went out, put a blanket over him, and then we got him buried.

******

Bought my son a young palomino mare over in Bisbee. Brought her home and started riding her, and my son was getting along pretty good with her...but she was a funny old girl. She'd get in a mood and buck you off in a heartbeat. And usually, we'd take and tie her to the bumper of my truck, and I'd go around the pasture a few times and let her lope, and then she was good for the rest of the day. She turned out to be one of the best ropers I ever roped on.

******

I remember when I was coaching Little League baseball. My son was on the team, and another friend of his was on the team, and they played Little League and went to the same high school. And later on, years later, he (my son's friend) came by the stable and needed a job, and I gave him a job for a while. And then he was with the stunt man's association, and he just needed a job until he could get back on the stunt man scene. Well, he worked for me for a little while, and then one day, he said that he had to leave. He had a part-time deal, and the next time I saw him, he had done a short, well, he did a spot on a movie called "Young Guns," and he was quite popular for a while. And then he went on to do other stunts and later came back to Phoenix. The last account I had of him, he was still out in Los Angeles doing stunts and stuff.

******

I remember also, when I was down in the Sierra Vista area, when I was coaching Little League...one time, one of the famed New York Yankees' short stop(s) was doing some National Guard, or whatever, type of reserve service at Fort Huachuca. And he came out to the Little League field, gave us a lot of pointers, shook hands with the kids and myself and some of the other coaches. And it was quite a thrill to see him and later on go turn on the TV and see him play for one of the most respected teams in the (professional) league.

******

Several years ago, I was invited by a friend down into Mexico, way down into Mexico, where they had a bunch of horses that they were selling off some of them. I went down there with him, and we met this gentleman who owned a ranch. And we got in a truck and started driving around his ranch, and looking at his stock and the horses that were for sale, I was really, really impressed. The ones they showed us and the ones that I wanted to buy, they were extremely good horse flesh and had been well trained, well broken. And they were all in good condition, and like I say, I wasn't expecting what I actually saw. But as we drove through the countryside and around, we saw all kinds of good livestock in Mexico, and one day, I want to go back there and buy some of their horses, because I see how well they take care of these horses and how well they were trained. And the people were extremely nice to us (as well).

******

Driving down the highway the other day, I recalled a deal where one of my friends, a stunt man in Phoenix, contacted me and wanted me to help him do a commercial up in Monument Valley for the Japanese. I set about to put everything together. They needed 18 horses and a couple of wranglers from me. We got it all together and went up to Monument Valley, and it was quite a deal. They paid for all the rooms and food and fed the horses. I had to take 18, as I've mentioned, and they had this deal set up…a tent where everyone ate—and it was open 24 hours a day. You could go there at any time of day or night and get steak and eggs, lobster, whatever you cared to have…it was available. This took 2 weeks. The wranglers were paid well, the horses were cared for real good, and 3 or 4 times a day, they'd run these horses across the Colorado River, and they would get shots of them going across the Colorado River. And sometimes the lighting wasn't right and everything, so the next day, you'd have to get up and do the same thing over again. They kept doing this for a period of approximately 7 to 10 days. And then, one day, when they were running the horses across the river, one of the ol' horses decided that he'd had enough and threw his tail over his back and took off at a hard run...and they couldn't catch him, couldn't locate him. Anyway, each horse was insured for $1500—that was the agreement when I sent them up–and when everything was done, and everyone was ready to come back, still no sign of the horse. So, the insurance company paid me for the horse, and everybody came back home and went about his business. I guess it was 2 to 3 weeks later that I got a call from a rancher near Monument

Valley, and he said, "Were you the gentleman who did the commercial up here sometime back?" I told him that I was, and he asked, "Were you missing a horse?" And I told him that I was, and he said, "Is it a bay gelding?" And I said, "Yes," and he said, "Well, I've got him right out here in my corrals. We picked him up out on the ranch a week or so ago, and you can come get him any time."" I made arrangements and sent somebody up and got the horse and brought him back to my place...notified the people who had the insurance on him, and they told me just to go ahead and keep the horse. So things wound up real good for me–I got paid for the horse and got to keep the horse...and it was a real good adventure, and I was glad to be a part of it.

******

The stunt man in Phoenix is a real good friend of mine. We've done a lot of shows together, including burning stage coaches, shoot-outs, trail rides, all types of adventurous things that we've done...and I'm seriously thinking about getting back into doing some of these things. And I certainly will call on my friend, the stunt man, here in Phoenix.

The Wigwam

I remember one time at the Wigwam Resort, they had a gold tournament with a lot of the NFL's famous quarterbacks. Then we had a cookout for them, of course, and got to get real up-close and talk to these gentlemen. And my (youngest) son got a lot of autographs, and this was a real nice time, as I do enjoy football, and I do enjoy a lot of the quarterbacks who were present at that time.

******

When I had another stable over in Scottsdale, one night we had a steak fry for the Phoenix Suns. They arrived in their buses and everything, kind of late in the evening...and by the time we got them all down to the cook-out area and got them settled in, security was so tight that you could barely get close to any of the players. But at least we got to see them all while they milled around and ate dinner. But to get up close and visit with them was almost impossible...but anyway, it was a great deal for us.

******

I recall another time when a famous celebrity visited the Wigwam, and we had the privilege of taking him on a hayride and putting on a skit with him. And it was, believe it or not, the real Lone Ranger. I recall I didn't have any white horses at the time, and we had to borrow one from my neighbor for him to use to do the skit on. And one of my wranglers dressed up like an Indian and rode a paint horse, and he was sup-posed to be Tonto. We got up to the hill-side, and everybody gathered and was sitting around...and after the meal was over, the Lone Ranger came up on the hill on this white horse and hollering, "Hi-ho, Silver!" And my wrangler was going, "Get 'em up, Scout," right behind him. And it brought back a lot of memories from over the years when I've watched him. And he was kind of my idol...and the amazing thing about this is that he was in his eighties at this time, and he still had the physique from back when it first started in the forties or fifties–forties, I do believe. This really brought back a lot of memories of all my movie days going to watch the Lone Ranger and Tonto.

******

For the last 11 years, we've brought in quite a bit of money over the years and helped a lot of crippled or sick children at St. Jude's (with what obviously became our Annual St. Jude's ride). But you know, without the horse, we would never have completed this deal. The ol' horses, they carry the people and go on this charity ride, and they go up into the mountains and back down from the mountains, through the rocks, over the hills, and they bring the people back. A donation (is) made, and we get the money for St. Jude's. However, I receive a letter and plaque from St. Jude's, thanking me for all I do for the organization over the years, but I have never received a letter saying thank the horses for all they did. And without these horses, there wouldn't be a ride, there'd be no donations coming in. But everybody forgets about that and thinks that I (or the people) did it. Of course, we had a lot to do with it, but again, without the horses, there would have been no St. Jude's ride. And there would have been no money for the crippled children.

******

Another nice time at the stable would occur every year, a couple of weeks before Christmas. The church in Litchfield Park would order 3 or 4 wagons–hay-wagons–to do Christmas caroling. We'd get our teams all cleaned up real good, and we'd put like, sleigh bells on the harness of the teams so that it would jingle when they were going down the streets. And they would all meet at the church, and we'd load all the wagons down, and each driver would go up a different street in Litchfield Park, and they would stop in front of houses and sing Christmas carols. You could sit there in the parking lot at the church and hear it all over Litchfield. It was a really great time and really gave you the Christmas spirit.

******

You know, it just seems I can't say enough good things about the Wigwam Resort. I was with them a long time, enjoyed every minute of it...(I) was treated well...a real top-notch organi-zation.

(So) keeping on the subject of the Wigwam, whilst I was operating the stable there, I recall some guests sending the general manager, Mr. Ravenswood, a letter saying how nice they were treated at the stable and that I ran a real good operation there. And I did later on receive a copy of a letter that Mr. Ravenswood had mailed to this particular guest, stating that I, Howard Green, didn't only have the best stable in Arizona, I had the best stable in the United States. And you know, that sure made me feel good...when somebody like the general man-ager of the resort will make that kind of state-ment. And it just makes you work even harder to please everyone.

******

I'd like to go back to the Wigwam one day. And with all my old friends, stunt people and part-time actors and all the people I know, I'd like to put on one great big show like we used to have there at the Wigwam. And I'd like to gather all these people and all the equipment–like the burning stagecoach, bucking barrel, roller-roper, and the bands, gun-fighters and everything. And (I'd like to) just put back, put on one great big show, just in memory of all the people I've worked with and all the good times we've had at the Wigwam Resort.

Random Thoughts

Got to let you in on a secret. A big old cowboy like me–I'm afraid of cats. I'm just paranoid about cats. One time, I took this girl home, it was her birthday, and we went inside and she got me a drink, and I'm sitting in a chair. And she said, "Just a minute, I want to show you what I got for my birthday." She went back into the room, came back out and had this...she just tossed this little white kitten into my lap. I went berserk. I threw the drink up into the air, I ran outside like a total idiot. And she didn't know that I was scared of cats–it really tore her up, and she was real sorry about the situation, although she didn't know. But she wasn't half as tore up as I was.

More on this cat situation...my friend was an animal control officer in southern Arizona, and I went with him one day. We were going out to look at a horse or something, I don't even recall, but we went in the animal control truck. We're driving along, and I could hear a faint "meow," and I said, "Tom, is there a cat in here?" And he said, "No, no there's no way a cat could be in here." We just kept driving, and after a while, I heard another little "meow," and I repeatedly asked him, "Are you sure? You know how I am about cats." He said, "I know, but I don't think there's any in here." So, we went a little further, and the "meow" got a little louder, and I grabbed the door handle–we were doing about 55, 60 mph, and I said, "Tom, pull this truck over, or I'm going to get out of this truck while it's still going." He whipped over to the side real quick, and I jumped out. And after searching the truck, there was a cat up underneath the dashboard, tangled up in wires. And he got the cat out and throwed it out, and I was kind of reluctant to get back in the truck again. But he told me, he said, "I've checked the whole truck, there aren't any more." So finally, I got back in the truck, and he's laughed at me ever since.

******

Enough on cats, back to the horse business. I have a policy that when I sell somebody a horse, I tell them right up front that if you don't get along with this horse, I will not give you your money back. However, I will replace the horse at no additional charge until you're satisfied. And that goes over real good...people say that you can't get a better guarantee than that, and I live by it. I have one girl that I've exchanged her horse at least 6 or 7 times–I don't even recall, it's been so many–and she will never be happy with any horse that you get her, but I will say this: she was the best publicity I could get. I sold more horses from her telling everybody how I kept my word and would come and exchange a horse when she wasn't happy with it. But I still go by those rules today, and I know I'm expecting a call any day that I've got to replace another horse for her. She's a beautiful lady, and she lives by her word, and I live by mine. She's helped me sell a lot of horses.

******

On Ted's last birthday
Liz was all set to dine
She ordered up food
And even some wine.

Old Ted was grinning
And having the time of his life
For his mind was on Tucson
And his first loving wife.

Ted said, "Liz, this may sound quite funny
I want to go to Tucson, but I need some money
And while me and my first wife are having a
meal
You take a shovel, and irrigate the field."

******

The other day, I was out on a ranch and got talking to the owner of it, and he was telling me that when they laid out the ranch it was laid out in 3 different counties. And the thought ran through my mind at the time that the county tax assessors must have had a field day. I'll bet there was more bickering and arguing on who was going to get the most money when it came to assess them for tax. You can just imagine what went on.

******

It was out in Buckeye in the early fall
Ted was bitching and moaning because he was
bald
Ted said it's time that he got a wig
As he rolled on the floor with his pot-bellied pig
Ted kept on griping and said, "This might
sound queer
But I think I would look good with a ring in my
ear."
So he drove off to town and returned with a
giggle
He said, "Look at my left ear, and watch my
ring wiggle."

******

One morning, at my stable, one of the girls didn't show up to take rides out. She didn't come in until the following day, and I asked her, "What happened? Why didn't you call? Why didn't you come in?" And she said, "Oh, we bought some new videos, and I had to stay home to watch them."

******

Coming down the freeway the other day, I spotted a huge accident. Several police cars and some other cars and traffic backed up. Later, I learned on the news that there were some fatalities, and when I returned home, I received a call from my (oldest) daughter that it was a neighbor who lived down the road that got burned beyond recognition. And it was quite a shock, because this lady used to board her horse with me...and later on, I received another call that they had animals that needed hay. So, I called and made arrangements for some hay to be delivered to these people at my cost, because knowing these people just live down the road...and knowing they had a lot of animals....knowing that they once kept their horse here...(it) kind of hit close to home. So, by making arrangements for the hay, I felt that I had helped a little, and I informed my daughter to let them know that if they had any other needs to please contact me.

******

The last stable I had, we were down kind of on the river bottom, down next to the river. And our trails went down by the river...and it was a beautiful riding area and plenty of it. One day, one of my riders came in and she was telling me that down there under a clump of trees and bushes, there were 2 chocolate Labrador dogs that run out and bark at the ride every time they go by. And she said that this has been going on for a while, and she'd just forgotten to tell me about it. Looking into the matter, somebody had dropped these 2 chocolate Labs off, 2 males they appeared to be, maybe a father and son...beautiful dogs, but under-nourished. I started going down where these dogs were and giving them a little bit of feed, just putting the feed a little closer to the stable every day. And then, at night, I would leave food out for them, out by the fence...and it wasn't long 'till I'd come in in the morning, and I'd see them sitting out in the bushes kind of waiting for feed. I continued doing this for several days, and then it wasn't long 'till these dogs were waiting for me outside the fence. They wouldn't come near me when I'd come in in the morning, but they would be waiting for their food. And I kept feeding the dogs, and the girls kind of sat down and started messing around with them...and they finally got to where we could pet them. And then, one day, a lady and her daughter came in to go on a ride. The lady didn't ride (the daughter went out with one of the guides) and she was telling me about her dog that had died, it was a Labrador...and I told her that she was in luck, because I had the replacement for her. So she went and looked at the dogs, and she couldn't get near the dogs, but one of the girls working there caught the older dog. She fell in love with it instantly, and when her daughter came back off her ride, she was just beside herself, so they wound up taking this dog home. And I know that he got a good home. And one of the girls that was working for me got friendly with the younger dog and wound up taking him home. And I do know that both of these dogs got a real good home, and I do know that when I come in the morning, I kind of miss seeing them waiting around the corner and looking for their food.

Conclusion

This book is rapidly coming to an end. I've almost got it finished and should have it off to be printed shortly, but just a word that I have one more book that I'm in the process of writing–it's called "The Long Trail from Arkansas to Arizona." And…just a preview of what it's about…it's about my life growing up, and about my trips to foreign countries, the people I came into contact with in Europe, Korea, Japan, (and) various other places. So, like I said, it'll be called, "The Long Trail from Arkansas to Arizona," and it should make for some real good reading, so watch for it, please!

You know, a lot of times when I'm off by myself and just kind of daydreaming, not really thinking about anything, just kind of hanging out, I often wondered what kind of job I would have liked to have through the course of my life. And when I'm through wondering what kind of job I would have like to have had, I find I've had the job I would like to have had, and I guess I'm still doing it...only on a smaller scale, because I'm not able to do a lot anymore. But I guess that's just the cowboy in me, that's all I've been, all I wanted to be, and I can't find anything else out there that even would half-way satisfy me compared to the job I have now. So, I guess I'll just wind down my trail and hang on to what I'm doing, because I like it better than anything I can think of, (even though) there's millions and millions of jobs and a hell of a lot better paying. I'm stuck, this is where I want to be, this is what I'm good at. I know damn well that I'm good at my job, and I've got a lot of people that can testify.

I've trained a lot of good horses, and there's some that I didn't do a good job on…but overall, the horses I've trained, the people were more than happy with them.

You know, it would be really interesting to know just how many people out there could make the statement that I just made and be honest about it. I'm going to bet you that you could count them all on one hand and have a couple of fingers left, because being out in this rat race every day–so, you make good money—what's good money if you're going to drop over dead worrying about it or fighting the traffic? I don't think it would be too many of them (that) could stand up and be honest like I am and really say they've been contented with their job for as many years as I have.

Back when I was growing up, I was told by a lot of people (that) if you live to be a hundred, you can count your friends on one hand and have 3 fingers left. Now, this sounds like a joke, but you get to looking around at your friends, your would-be friends, fair-weather friends, whatever the case may be. But look around and see just how many friends that you'd've got if you were down and that would come and pick you up instead of kicking you in the teeth. You look around and check that out, and I'm sure that you'll find a lot of truth in this like I have. Years ago, I got into some trouble, needed friends. At the time I got into trouble, I had friends all around me, but when I started calling and really needed friends, one person came to my aid. And I guarantee you, he proved that he was a real true friend. Unfortunately, he's dead now, but he was the only one who came to my rescue, and I'll never forget it.

I worked for a gentlemen one time who told me (that) it didn't matter how broke you were, when you were around people, you should act like you've got all the money you need…because nobody wants to be associated with a loser. So, never let people know what your financial situation is, and just go right ahead as if you have all the money you need, and good things will happen from this.

******

···

I've been pretty sick for the last few days and don't know how much longer it's going to go on...having no one else to turn to buy my wife. And she came through with flying colors...hauling hay, feeding all the animals, taking care of all the things here at the house to do...plus taking care of me. And I'm greatly indebted to her, and she's been all I ever hoped for her to be.

I have 5 children, by 2 different marriages, and they've all grown up and made a life of their own...doing quite well. My 2 youngest ones are both at university and due to graduate soon, and I'm looking forward to seeing what trail they'll take when their days at school are over.

The way I've looked at life, if you can hang around long enough to see all of your children grown and making a good living for themselves and not having to depend on home...then I feel that I did it. I feel that I've accomplished my mission, and anything on down the road will be pure gravy.

Looking back at my life and the things I've done that I was able to do, and the people I was able to meet...there might have been some things that I would have changed a little bit, got more out of. But all in all, I'm happy with what happened, and (I) probably wouldn't change anything if I had the chance.

You know how when you pick up your reins and are riding down the trail...I guess you could call it the twilight trail, 'cause I've had more, I've got more that I've done in the past than I will ever get done in the future.... So, the old saying goes that you never look back–look straight ahead and take advantage of what you've got.

Ride on down the trail hoping there'll be a good tomorrow.

....

Life goes on now. I'm getting tired. I've been weak. I've been not feeling well for a long time. Hopefully, things will get better. But as I ride on down the trail towards my last round-up, I know that I will leave a lot of knowledge out back here...and I hope that everybody–well, not everybody—but I hope there'll be people who will take advantage of my knowledge whenever they read this book.

Through my long lifetime here on earth, there were stressful times. There were good times. I guess it was meant to be this way. I've dealt with a lot of nice people, and I've dealt with a lot of people that's not so nice. I think I've carried more stress than I've had good times in my life, and as I head on down to the last round-up–I might even say, the big feed-lot in the sky–there might be greener pastures on the other side of the mountain. I'll just have to go and see. But all in all, I hope I can go out of this world without any regrets...and just maybe, there'll be a place on the other side of the mountain for an old cowboy like me. But Happy Trails. So long, folks. Hope to see you in my next book. Adios.

All Around Cowboy

I met a heap of cowboys
And some was real top hands.
I saw a million cattle
And read a lot of brands.
I've seen some hard old winters,
When nearly all the cattle died.
I've rode some cutting horses
That would turn right out of their hides.
I ate my share of beefsteak
And drunk some whisky, too.
Did a little dancing,
Wasn't nothing else to do.

Been bucked off old Outlaw,
Said I couldn't start to ride
And saw some fine old buddies
Go over the Great Divide.
With friends and family,
Now I'm making my last stand,
And hoping to be on horseback
When I reach the Promised Land.

••

0-595-26521-9